MW01089566

Italianamerican

Italianamerican
The Scorsese Family Cookbook

CATHERINE SCORSESE with Georgia Downard

Random House   New York

Copyright © 1996 by Catherine Scorsese

All rights reserved under International and Pan-American Copyright
Conventions. Published in the United States by Random House, Inc.,
New York, and simultaneously in Canada by Random House of Canada Limited, Toronto.

Grateful acknowledgment is made to the following for permission to reprint previously
published or broadcast material:

Faber and Faber Limited: Excerpts from *GoodFellas,* by Martin Scorsese and Nicholas Pileggi,
and *Casino,* by Martin Scorsese and Nicholas Pileggi, published by Faber and Faber
Limited. Reprinted by permission of Faber and Faber Limited.

National Broadcasting Company, Inc.: Brief excerpt from an appearance by Martin Scorsese
on *Late Night with David Letterman* from 1991. Copyright © 1991 by National Broadcasting
Company, Inc. All rights reserved. Courtesy of National Broadcasting Company, Inc.

Thunder's Mouth Press: Excerpt from *Martin Scorsese: A Journey,* by Mary Pat Kelly. Copyright
© 1991 by Mary Pat Kelly. Reprinted by permission of Thunder's Mouth Press.

ISBN 0-679-44282-0

Random House website address: http://www.randomhouse.com/

Printed in the United States of America on acid-free paper
98765432
Book design by Wynn Dan
First Edition

For my husband, Charlie

CONTENTS

Italianamerican

INTRODUCTION:
THE PASTA SAUCE

"The Italians of my parents' generation are held
together by the notion of the family. That is why the pasta sauce is so
sacred to the Italian family." MARTIN SCORSESE

COOKING LESSONS

MARTIN SCORSESE: How did you learn to make the sauce?

CATHERINE SCORSESE: When you first get married, you're really not much of a cook. I watched my mother make sauce. I watched my mother-in-law. I got a lot from my mother-in-law, a lot from the family.

CHARLES SCORSESE: She got more from my mother than from her mother.

CATHERINE SCORSESE: See, there he goes again, putting his mother in.

CHARLES SCORSESE: They were two different cooks. Her mother had nine children. Some kids didn't like certain things, and she used to satisfy them in different ways. My mother-in-law was a good cook, but she couldn't cook the way she wanted to. Beginning with her husband, my father-in-law. He used to cook for himself, so he was giving a bad example right there.

Charles and Catherine Scorsese in *Italianamerican*, 1974.

CATHERINE SCORSESE *(making the pasta sauce)*: My mother taught me one way and my mother-in-law had a different plan to cooking. She was a very good cook. I ended up cooking this way to please him more. That's the truth.

This is what my mother-in-law taught me: Take a few spoonfuls of tomato and throw them in [the pot] because the meatballs have to remain very soft. Not like the meatballs you eat sometimes when you're invited somewhere. They're as hard as can be. You throw them at the wall, the wall will crack. I really shouldn't say that because I have a lot of friends and I'll be getting a lot of telephone calls.

(Italianamerican)

Tomato Sauce with Meat

1 large onion, minced

2 tablespoons olive oil

3 cans (28 ounces each) whole tomatoes in thick puree

2 cans (16 ounces each) tomato sauce

2 cups water

1 can (6 ounces) tomato paste

3 large cloves garlic, peeled

2 carrots, peeled

1 potato, peeled

3 tablespoons each minced fresh basil and parsley
      leaves, or 1 tablespoon each dried, crumbled

Salt to taste

Cayenne pepper to taste

$\frac{1}{4}$ cup fresh bread crumbs

$\frac{1}{4}$ cup milk

6 ounces each ground pork, veal, and beef

1 large egg, lightly beaten

$\frac{1}{4}$ cup freshly grated Parmesan

2 tablespoons each minced fresh basil and parsley
      leaves, or $1\frac{1}{2}$ teaspoons each dried, crumbled

In a large saucepan or casserole set over moderate heat, cook the onion in the oil, stirring occasionally, for 5 minutes.

In a blender or food processor, puree the tomatoes and sauce. Add the tomato mixture to the pan along with the water, tomato paste, garlic, carrots, potato, basil, parsley, and salt and cayenne. Bring to a boil and simmer, stirring occasionally, partially covered, for 30 minutes.

In a small bowl, soak the bread crumbs in the milk until softened.

In a large bowl, combine the bread-crumb mixture with the meat, egg, Parmesan, basil, parsley, salt, cayenne, and ½ cup of the sauce. Add the meat to the sauce, shredding it and dropping it in a little at a time. Simmer the sauce, partially covered, stirring occasionally, for 1 hour. Before serving remove the garlic cloves, carrots, and potato.

Makes about 12 cups   Recipe Catherine Scorsese

Martin, Catherine, and Charles Scorsese at home in Little Italy.

SICILY:

FAMILY RECIPES

"My mother never used a recipe. All the old folks cooked like that.
They never used measurements. If it came good, it came good.
If it didn't, too bad." CATHERINE SCORSESE

POLIZZI GENEROSA
(the Sicilian hometown of the Scorsese family)

Historians have several theories about Polizzi's name, but none have anything to do with generous police.

- In early medieval times it was a city of the king, a "basileopolis," a name that may have melted into "Polizzi."
- Polizzi is the namesake of Castor and Pollux, collectively known as the "Palaci" gods.
- It was the "Polis Iside," the city of Isis. A marble statue of the Egyptian goddess was found there in 1650 in the ruins of an ancient temple. It was smashed to bits by a Capuchin monk in the eighteenth century. Her framed image still hangs in the stores of the town.

But it was Frederick II, the European emperor who made Sicily his capital, who added "Generosa" to the town's name in 1234, because of the town's generosity to him and his army. He was fighting wars in northern Italy and Central Europe; Polizzi supplied him with arms, men, horses, and grain.

(Theresa Maggio)

Polizzi Generosa, 1996.

THE SCORSESE FAMILY

CHARLES SCORSESE: My father and mother came from Sicily, di Palermo—from a town called Polizzi Generosa. When my father was a little boy, about six or seven years old, his mother had died, his father remarried and somehow or another—I don't know what happened—he didn't want to stay there and some man took him in. He had a farm with goats and things like that, and he would work for this man. At nineteen, my father was coming to this country but this man didn't want him to come over here. He wanted him to marry one of his daughters, but my father said, "No. I'm going to America."

It was around 1901, something like that. He started to work as a laborer. When he was twenty-one, he decided he wanted to get married and he went to my mother and he married her, right here in the old St. Patrick's Church.

During World War I, my father went to work on ships. They had him down in the hull. Half the time, they wouldn't even let him come up, because they figured if these people came up, they wouldn't want to work under those conditions. They used to give them food and everything else down there. And he finally wanted to work for New York Steam. Without an education, he worked for New York Steam and had a hundred people working for him.

Then he went into business. He had, I'd say, about eight, nine, or ten businesses. All fruit and vegetables. And every one he put up, he lost money on. But he kept trying. One day, he said, "I bought the grocery store downstairs." We were all furious. We didn't want him to get into business. The New York Steam people came over to see him, they wanted him back. He wouldn't go back. He said, "I got my own business and that's it." My father always told me, any time you're in business, you can owe all the money in the world, but you always got money in your pocket. You can always support a family. The bills, you paid them as they came along. Finally, after so many years, he lost his business—just at the time when the Second World War started.

As far as my mother goes, well, she was a strong woman. My father would never get into arguments with anybody, she would face them. She was a very strong woman, even with us, with the children. When she told you something, that was it. You couldn't answer her. She was tough. When she came over here, she almost died on that trip. The boats

Teresa and Francesco Scorsese on their wedding day.

were small, very small. It took over a month to get here. They didn't think they were going to make it.

When I was a little boy, we had two boarders that lived with us. My mother used to cook for them, wash their clothes, and they used to pay her. There were nine people in four rooms counting the kitchen. Small rooms, there was no such thing as elaborate rooms. We had no furniture then. You had beds. In the daytime, you'd pick them up and you had the room. In the nighttime you'd fold them down and go to sleep.

(*Italianamerican*)

ONE BIG FAMILY IN NEW YORK

CHARLES SCORSESE: It was like one big house. People used to leave their doors open. You'd go in. . . If I didn't like what my mother used to cook, I'd go downstairs and eat. I used to go upstairs: "Mama, what are you cooking?" If I didn't like it—downstairs. We used to be one big family. It's different now.

Catherine Scorsese

241 Elizabeth Street, where Charles Scorsese grew up, 1996. The front door has been replaced.

BRACIOLE

Six 6-ounce slices round steak, pounded very thin
Salt and pepper to taste

For the stuffing:
1 cup toasted bread crumbs
2 hard-cooked eggs, finely chopped
6 slices salami, finely chopped
¼ cup freshly grated Locatelli
4 cloves garlic, minced
2 tablespoons minced parsley leaves
Salt and pepper to taste

2 tablespoons olive oil

Pat the meat dry and season with salt and pepper.

Make the stuffing: In a bowl, combine all the ingredients.

Spread a thin layer of the stuffing on each slice of the meat, roll up the meat to enclose the stuffing, and tie with string.

In a large skillet set over moderate heat, heat the oil until hot. Add the meat and cook until it is browned on all sides. Transfer to a plate.

Add the braciole to tomato sauce (recipe on page 90) and simmer for $1\frac{1}{2}$ hours, or until tender.

Makes 6   Recipe Teresa Scorsese

Macaroni with Lamb and Veal in White Sauce: "Charlie loved this. It was his mother's dish. He used to tell me: 'Make it like my mother made it.'"

MACARONI WITH LAMB AND VEAL IN WHITE SAUCE

1½ pounds lamb shoulder, cut into 2-inch pieces
1½ pounds veal shank (osso bucco cut),
    cut 1½ inches thick
4 tablespoons olive oil
Salt and freshly ground black pepper to taste
1 large onion, sliced
¼ teaspoon sugar
3 red potatoes, peeled and halved
4 cups chicken stock or broth
3 tablespoons minced fresh parsley leaves
1 pound perciatelli
Freshly grated Locatelli to taste

In a casserole, combine the lamb and veal with enough cold water to cover by 2 inches. Bring the liquid to a boil and simmer for 10 minutes. Drain, rinse, and pat dry the meat.

In the casserole, set over moderate heat, heat 2 tablespoons of the oil until hot. Add the meat and salt and pepper and brown the meat on all sides. Transfer the meat to a platter.

Add the onion and sugar to the casserole and cook, stirring occasionally, until golden. Transfer the onion to the platter. Add 2 tablespoons oil to the casserole and heat it until hot. Add the potatoes and cook them until golden on all sides. Transfer the potatoes to a bowl and reserve.

Return the meat and onion to the casserole, add the chicken stock or broth, enough water to cover the meat by 2 inches, parsley, salt, and pepper. Bring the liquid to a boil and simmer it, partially covered, for $1\frac{1}{2}$ hours. Add the potatoes and cook for an additional 30 minutes, or until the meat and potatoes are tender.

With a slotted spoon, transfer the meat and potatoes to a large plate and keep warm. Reduce the cooking liquid until slightly thickened. Correct the seasoning, adding salt and pepper to taste.

Meanwhile, cook the perciatelli according to package directions, drain, and transfer it to a large bowl.

Strain enough of the sauce over the pasta to coat it, add the cheese, and toss to combine. Arrange the meat and vegetables on a platter and serve separately with a mixed green salad.

Serves 4 to 6   Recipe Teresa Scorsese

MIXED GREEN SALAD

1 head romaine lettuce
1 cucumber, peeled and sliced
2 to 3 plum tomatoes, cored and cut into small wedges
1 small red onion, sliced thin
Olive oil and red wine vinegar to taste
Salt and pepper to taste

Tear the lettuce leaves into bite-size pieces and transfer them to a large salad bowl. Add the cucumber, tomatoes, and onion. Sprinkle with the oil, vinegar, and salt and pepper, and toss to combine.

Serves 4 to 6

CHRISTMAS DINNER

CHARLES SCORSESE: I never remember a Christmas tree in my mother's house. They didn't go in for it, the old folks. What they believed in was that at twelve o'clock at night they went to church, they celebrated Mass, and after that they came home. We had some sausage and things like that at the church, and the next day we had a big dinner with the family.

The next generation: Charles, Catherine, and Martin Scorsese with their tree.

STUFFED LOBSTER TAILS

**2 lobster tails, split lengthwise down the flesh side, the
     shell lightly flattened**
**1 can (16 ounces) whole tomatoes, chopped, with their
     liquid reserved**
4 cloves garlic, minced fine
2 tablespoons minced fresh parsley
1 teaspoon red pepper flakes
1 tablespoon olive oil
Salt to taste

Preheat the oven to 400 degrees F. Arrange the lobster tails
in an oiled baking dish.

In a bowl, combine the tomatoes, garlic, parsley, pepper
flakes, oil, and salt. Spoon the mixture over the lobster.

Bake the lobster, basting occasionally, for 20 to 25 minutes,
or until just cooked through.

Serves 2   Recipe Catherine Scorsese

CALAMARI, SCUNGILLI, AND SHRIMP SALAD

1½ pounds calamari (squid), cleaned, tentacles and
 flaps removed, body sacs cut crosswise into
 ¼-inch-wide rings
1 pound shrimp, shelled and deveined
3 cans (6½ ounces each) scungilli (conch), drained,
 rinsed, and patted dry
1½ cups minced celery
4 large cloves garlic, minced fine, or to taste
1 cup pitted black olives, halved
1 cup green olives with pimiento, halved
Salt and freshly ground black pepper to taste
⅓ to ½ cup fresh lemon juice, or to taste
½ cup olive oil, or to taste
⅓ cup minced fresh parsley leaves

In a saucepan of boiling salted water, cook the calamari and
shrimp for 3 minutes, or just until opaque and tender.

Calamari, Scungilli, and Shrimp Salad.

Drain and pat dry.

In a large bowl, combine the calamari, shrimp, scungilli, celery, garlic, olives, and salt and pepper. Chill the mixture, covered, until ready to serve.

In a small bowl, whisk together the lemon juice, oil, and salt and pepper. Add the dressing to the seafood mixture along with the parsley and toss to combine. Correct the seasoning.

Serves 8 to 10   Recipe Fanny di Giovanni

TERESA SCORSESE'S
ITALIAN COOKIES

1 pound unsalted butter, softened

1¼ cups sugar

4 teaspoons vanilla extract

6 large eggs

6 to 7 cups all-purpose flour

2 tablespoons baking powder

½ cup sifted confectioners' sugar

1 teaspoon ground cinnamon, or to taste

In a bowl with an electric beater, cream the butter and sugar until light and fluffy. Beat in the vanilla extract. Add the eggs, one at a time, and beat until combined well.

Into a bowl, sift the flour and baking powder. Add the flour to the butter mixture, 1 cup at a time, beating well after each addition until a soft but not sticky dough is formed. Wrap the dough in plastic and chill for 1 hour.

Preheat the oven to 350 degrees F. Removing ½ cup chilled dough at a time, roll it out into a rope 12 inches long. With fingertips, gently press the rope into a ¼-inch thickness, and with a French fry cutter cut diagonally into 2-inch pieces.

Arrange the cookies 1 inch apart on an ungreased baking sheet and bake for 12 to 15 minutes, or until lightly golden around the edges. Transfer the cookies to racks to cool.

In a bowl, combine the confectioners' sugar with the cinnamon, then transfer the mixture to a fine sieve. Gently sprinkle over the cookies. Store in airtight containers.

Makes about 6 dozen

THE FAMILY

CHARLES SCORSESE: Our fathers and mothers, they came from a different world. They brought us up that as long as we ate and were healthy, then that's all that counted. They couldn't afford to send us to school, they didn't have that kind of money. It was all they had to do to survive. Thank God that my mother and father, they reached to see us all get married and settle up nice families.

Francesco and Teresa Scorsese's fiftieth wedding anniversary (they are seated in the middle row, second and third from the right).

THE CAPPA FAMILY

CATHERINE SCORSESE: My parents were from the town of
Ciminna. My father didn't know who his mother was. He
had been on his own, so he went to live with some family.
They took him in, then when he came of age he went away
to be a soldier in the cavalry.

One day they were coming through my mother's town. Of
course, everybody comes out on the balconies to look at the
soldiers going by. My father wore a blue uniform with a hat
with a big white plume on it and he was on horseback. My
mother was on the balcony, and when he passed by, he
looked at her and she looked at him and it was sort of love at
first sight. He said that the balcony was so low that if she just
put her hand down she could touch him. Of course, they
fell in love. So they courted for about twenty-two days and
then they got married.

My sister was about six months old and my father kept
asking my mother to come to America. But she didn't want
to come. She was afraid of the boat. He would tell her: "It's
nice over here. It will be a different life." Finally he got so
mad, he wrote her, "If you don't come to America, I'm

Domenica Cappa.

Martin Cappa.

going to leave you." So she got on the next boat. But she didn't want to, so her brother tricked her that he was going with her. She turned around for a second and he just faded out of sight. She became frantic. But it was too late, the boat had started.

It was a very bad trip. They looked liked peasants, you know, my little sister with the little kerchief on her head. They came to America and went to live on Third Street, then on Elizabeth Street. Eventually my aunt came. There was no place to live, so they took in my aunt, my uncle, and her son. That's fourteen people. My aunt occupied the bedroom, the kitchen was in the middle, and my mother and father and the [nine] children were in the living room.

My father was a scaffold maker. He made scaffolds—the board that's outside of the buildings that they stand on. Of course, it was hard to get work here. So wherever they could get work, they would go. I remember him going to Springfield, New Jersey. He would leave on a Monday morning and come back Friday night. For forty-five dollars a week. At that time, it was big money. He was supporting nine children.

My father had handlebars. So one night on a Friday, there was a knock at the door, we opened the door and all of a sudden we ran back and were pulling on my mother. "What's the matter?" she said. I said, "There's a man at the door." It was my father. He had shaved off his handlebars. He used to get a big charge out of things like that.

One time he hurt his arm and he was out of work for so long. When the master of the house wasn't working, it was hard on us. My mother used to sew pants to keep the family going. She made pants for Daddy Browning, a millionaire. He married a young girl named Peaches. He used to go to Arnheim on Ninth Street to have his clothes made and they used to give the pants to my mother because her sewing was beautiful.

She used to teach us how to sew. We had to sit by her and do the seams up. And [watch] the children. Who was running around, who was wet, who was hungry, who we had to give a bottle to. That's how we were raised.

(Italianamerican)

Catherine Scorsese

CAPONATINA SICILIANA
(Eggplant, Olive, and Celery Appetizer)

2 large eggplants

Salt to taste

1 jar (6½ ounces) oil-cured black olives, pitted and
    halved

1 jar (5¾ ounces) green olives with pimiento, drained
    and halved

1 jar (3 ounces) capers, drained

4 large stalks celery, diced

½ to ⅔ cup olive oil

2 large onions, sliced

2 cans (16 ounces each) tomato sauce

Freshly ground pepper to taste

¼ cup sugar

½ cup red wine vinegar

Trim the eggplants, cut them into 1-inch cubes, and transfer them to a colander. Sprinkle with salt and let them stand for 30 minutes. Rinse, drain well, and pat dry.

In a bowl, combine the black olives, green olives, and capers. Cover with warm water and let them plump for 20 minutes. Drain well.

In a saucepan of boiling water, blanch the celery for 1 to 2 minutes, or until just tender. Drain and pat dry.

In a large skillet set over moderately high heat, heat 3 table-spoons of the oil until hot. Add the eggplant in small batches and cook it, stirring occasionally and adding 3 to 4 table-spoons of water to prevent sticking, until just tender and golden brown. Transfer the fried eggplant to a bowl and, adding oil and water as needed, fry the remaining eggplant.

Add 2 tablespoons of oil to the skillet and heat it until hot over moderate heat. Add the onions and cook, stirring occa-sionally, just until tender.

Add the tomato sauce, 2 cups of water, the reserved egg-plant, olives, capers, celery, and salt and pepper. Simmer the mixture over low heat, stirring occasionally, for 30 minutes.

In a small bowl, combine the sugar and vinegar, stirring until dissolved. Add the sugar mixture to the eggplant mixture and stir to combine. Transfer the caponatina to a bowl, let it cool to room temperature, and chill it, covered, for 1 to 2 days to allow the flavors to blend.

Serves 8 to 10   Recipe Domenica Cappa

VARIATION

There's another way of preparing this. You can put a little bit of tuna fish on top of the eggplant. You can eat it with a fork or in a sandwich. It's the most delicious thing.

Stuffed Breast of Veal

A 5-pound boned breast of veal with pocket
Salt and pepper to taste

For the stuffing:
1 sweet potato (8 ounces), peeled and diced
1 small white potato (4 ounces), peeled and diced
1 small carrot, peeled and diced
2 stalks celery, diced
½ cup minced onion
½ pound ground pork
4 tablespoons olive oil
½ cup cooked rice
¼ cup grated Locatelli
2 hard-cooked eggs, chopped
2 tablespoons minced fresh parsley
Salt and pepper to taste

Olive oil to taste
Paprika to taste

Preheat the oven to 350 degrees F. Rinse the veal and pat dry. Season with salt and pepper.

Make the stuffing : In a saucepan of boiling salted water, blanch the sweet potato, white potato, carrot, celery, and onion for 2 minutes. Drain and pat dry.

In a skillet set over moderate heat, cook the pork in 1 tablespoon of oil, stirring, just until no longer pink. Transfer it to a bowl and let cool.

Add the blanched vegetables, the remaining oil, rice, cheese, eggs, parsley, and salt and pepper to the pork and stir to combine well. Fill the pocket with stuffing and seal by sewing up or securing with toothpicks.

Arrange the veal on a rack in a roasting pan, brush with oil, and season with paprika, salt, and pepper. Add enough water to measure 1 inch in the pan and roast, covered with foil, for $2\frac{1}{2}$ hours. Remove the foil and continue to roast, basting with pan juices, for 30 minutes more.

Transfer the veal to a cutting board and let it stand, loosely covered, for 10 minutes before slicing.

Serves 8   Recipe Domenica Cappa

KATIE'S TIP

We used to put strips of salami, a sliced egg, and pieces of Provolone cheese inside the veal. That would give it a really nice taste.

PASTA DOUGH

CATHERINE SCORSESE: I used to buy the dough, put it in the freezer, and then when I needed it, I used to take it out, let it rise. A lot of people have no patience. I can't wait that long.

FANNY DI GIOVANNI (Charles Scorsese's sister): I remember you used to have to put it in towels on the bed.

CATHERINE SCORSESE: And I remember one night, when my mother was making macaroni, the kids were playing in the bedroom. They didn't know there was dough on the bed and they got into bed. My mother couldn't use the dough because the kids were sleeping on it. She wanted to kill them because there were a few children on the bed—we were four boys and five girls. But we got a beating.

FANNY DI GIOVANNI: A good way of kneading the dough . . .

CATHERINE SCORSESE: We had a lot of fun when we were kids. We used to get in trouble a lot. Nine children, and there were always people that wanted to come and sleep in our house. Where the hell are we gonna put them? we wondered.

Pasta with Spinach and Potatoes

⅔ cup olive oil

1 large potato, peeled and cut into small cubes

Salt and pepper to taste

1 cup minced onion

2 pounds fresh spinach, trimmed, washed well, and
    drained

1¼ cups water

1 cup tomato sauce

½ cup fresh bread crumbs

2 large cloves garlic, minced

1 tablespoon minced fresh parsley

1 pound linguini

Freshly grated Locatelli or Parmesan to taste

In a skillet set over moderately high heat, heat ¼ cup of the oil until hot. Add the potato cubes and salt and pepper, and cook, stirring occasionally, until golden brown. Transfer the potato cubes to a plate. Add ¼ cup of the oil to the pan and cook the onion, stirring occasionally, for 5 minutes, or until golden. Add the spinach and ¼ cup of the water and cook, stirring, until wilted. Stir in the potatoes, tomato sauce, and 1 cup water and simmer for 20 minutes, or until the potatoes and spinach are tender.

In a skillet set over moderate heat, heat the remaining oil. Add the bread crumbs and garlic and cook, stirring, until golden. Transfer them to a bowl and stir in the parsley.

In a large saucepan of boiling salted water, cook the linguini until al dente, drain, and return to the pan. Add the spinach and potato mixture and gently toss just to combine. Transfer to a serving dish and sprinkle with the bread crumbs. Serve with the cheese.

Serves 4 to 6   Recipe Domenica Cappa

SICILIAN CAKE

2 pounds ricotta, drained well
¾ cup sugar
2 cups heavy cream
2 teaspoons vanilla extract
¼ cup dark rum
1 can (20 ounces) crushed pineapple, drained well
3 packages ladyfingers
Chopped walnuts, semisweet chocolate chips, and
   glacéed cherries for garnish

In a large bowl with an electric beater, beat the ricotta and sugar until combined well. Add the heavy cream, vanilla, and rum and continue to beat until thick and smooth. Stir in the pineapple.

Line the bottom and sides of a buttered 9-inch springform pan with some of the ladyfingers, top with one third of the filling, and cover with half the remaining ladyfingers. Add half the remaining filling, cover with the rest of the ladyfingers, and top with the last of the filling. Sprinkle with walnuts, chocolate chips, and glacéed cherries. Cover the cake with plastic and chill overnight.

Run a knife around the inside of the pan and release the sides. Transfer the cake to a serving dish.

Makes one 9-inch cake   Recipe Domenica Cappa

The Cappa family: Catherine with her parents and older sister, Sara.

SAINT JOSEPH'S DAY

CATHERINE SCORSESE: Then there was a dish that they ate only on Saint Joseph's Day, March 19—it was a special feast day. No meat was eaten, only fish. Perciatelli with a sauce that was made of bread crumbs and anchovies. It was delicious. A lot of people used to make it in the building, and you used to see the people come out with the dishes. You could smell it throughout the house.

SAINT JOSEPH PASTA

1 cup minced onion

½ cup olive oil

2 cans (230 grams each) Condimento Completo per
      Pasta con Sarde

2 cups tomato sauce

½ cup water

1 pound perciatelli

2 cups fresh bread crumbs

2 tablespoons freshly grated Locatelli or Parmesan

1 large clove garlic, finely minced

Cayenne pepper to taste

Salt to taste

In a saucepan set over moderate heat, cook the onion in 2 tablespoons of oil for 3 minutes, stirring occasionally, until softened. Add the Condimento, tomato sauce, and water, bring to a boil, and simmer, stirring occasionally, for 20 minutes.

Preheat the oven to 400 degrees F.

Meanwhile, in a large saucepan of boiling salted water, cook the perciatelli until just tender and drain.

In a large skillet set over moderate heat, heat the remaining oil until hot. Add the bread crumbs and cook, stirring, until golden brown. Transfer them to a bowl and add the cheese, garlic, cayenne, and salt.

In a large bowl, combine the pasta with enough sauce to just coat. Transfer it to an oiled baking dish and sprinkle with enough of the bread-crumb mixture to lightly cover the top. Bake for 15 minutes. Serve the remaining sauce and bread crumbs separately.

Serves 6   Recipe Domenica Cappa

Saint Joseph Pasta.

LITTLE ITALY:
LIFE ON
ELIZABETH STREET

"You never had to leave the neighborhood. We had
everything there: the pork shop, the cheese shop, the barber,
the funeral parlor . . ." MARTIN SCORSESE

THE NEIGHBORHOOD

CHARLES SCORSESE: First it was all Irish. Then the Italian people came in. And there was a lot of Jewish business around here. There was a little five-and-ten-cent store, there was a shoe store, a dry-goods store—like Orchard Street is today. It was crowded. As far as the neighborhood here and Delancey Street, and Orchard Street, Jewish and Italians all worked together. We used to amuse ourselves eating. Going to different restaurants. At that time it was cheap. We went to Houston Street for potato knishes and a cup of coffee. A dime. Yonah Schimmel's, I used to go there.

CATHERINE SCORSESE: Naturally the neighborhood people would come down to shop.

CHARLES SCORSESE: I'll never forget—the pushcarts in the morning were on this side [of the street] because there was no sun. In the afternoon when the sun came on this side, the pushcarts shifted over to the other side. You couldn't get a store over here. Every store, every basement was taken. Because you had lemon dealers. At the time, we used to get lemons from Europe. Lemons, oranges, all kinds of fruit. There was one, two, three, four different places with all that stuff around here. I don't know what happened. They faded away. There was sort of a depression and people started moving away.

The kids all used to steal. For fun sometimes. They'd take something on the pushcart, make the guy chase them, and the rest of the kids used to go and pick stuff from the cart. Kids' stuff, that's all it was. But sometimes it was that you needed that stuff. Your mother and father couldn't afford to get you anything. A kid used to grab something and use it. Fruit or a piece of crockery or something like that.

MARTIN SCORSESE: Were the Chinese here when you first came?

CHARLES SCORSESE: Chinatown was confined on the other side of Canal Street.

CATHERINE SCORSESE: People were afraid to walk through it. You used to hear stories about it and all of them true.

CHARLES SCORSESE: Years ago they used to have tong wars. I

remember them as a kid. You had detectives, two on each corner.

CATHERINE SCORSESE: In other words, it was dangerous.

CHARLES SCORSESE: Not to us. Amongst themselves.

MARTIN SCORSESE: How about the Irish?

CHARLES SCORSESE: When the Italian people came here, the Irish resented it because they didn't want to be thrown out of their own neighborhood. They used to have six, seven bars over here. All Irish bars.

CATHERINE SCORSESE: First they resented the Italians. But then everybody got together and they made one big happy family. They sort of got used to the idea. But in the beginning it was a little tough. It's just like everything else.

(Italianamerican)

Mulberry Street, looking north toward Canal Street, 1900.

CATHERINE AND CHARLES

Catherine Cappa and Charles Scorsese were born in 1912
and 1913, respectively, on Elizabeth Street, where the Sicilians lived.
The Neapolitans lived on Mulberry Street.

CATHERINE SCORSESE: Sixty years I was married to Charlie. He was a gem. He was so handsome.

GEORGIA DOWNARD: How did you meet him?

CATHERINE SCORSESE: He lived across the street from me and used to go to see his sister, who lived on the third floor; we lived right above her. He kept coming up, coming up. I used to see him in the building and I asked, "Who the hell is this guy?" One day I was talking to the sister and she told me, "Oh, that's my brother. He likes to stay with me."

He played the guitar and tried to make me notice him. I thought, "What a show-off. He doesn't even know how to play that guitar and look at him." This went on for weeks.

One night he took me to the movies on Second Avenue and Tenth Street. He came with this package. "I've got

The wedding of Catherine Cappa and Charles Scorsese.

something for you," he said. I couldn't wait to get home because I wanted to see what was in that gift box. When I opened up the box there was a beautiful brown wool dress with a little leopard collar. "I just felt like buying it for you," he told me. He was so sweet. I went inside and put it on, and when I came out, he said, "Looks nice on you. I'm going to take it for you." I wanted to tell him, "Make sure you pay for it." And that's my life. It was a wonderful life.

GEORGIA DOWNARD: What was your wedding like?

CATHERINE SCORSESE: It was in June. My mother had no room. The apartment was small, so we had the party on the roof of the building.

MINESTRONE

1½ cups finely chopped onion

1½ cups finely chopped carrot

2 tablespoons olive oil

2 cans (19 ounces each) red kidney beans,
     including liquid

1 can (19 ounces) chickpeas, including liquid

2 cups water

4 cups chicken stock or broth

1 cup drained, chopped tomato

Salt and pepper to taste

1 cup tubettini or other small pasta, cooked al dente

In a casserole set over moderate heat, cook the onion and carrot in the oil, stirring occasionally, for 5 minutes. Add the kidney beans, chickpeas, water, stock, tomato, and salt and pepper. Bring the liquid to a boil and simmer, covered, for 20 minutes.

Add the tubettini and simmer until heated through.

Serves 10 to 12   Recipe Catherine Scorsese

WEDDING DINNER
IN HONOR OF
MR. & MRS. PETER LOGERFO
HOTEL DELMONICO · SEPT. 29 · 1946

Delmonico's Hotel: Charles and Catherine Scorsese at a wedding party, 1946 (left center table: Catherine, wearing pearls, is to the right of Charles).

Macaroni with Lamb and Veal in Tomato Sauce

2 lamb shanks, about $2\frac{1}{2}$ pounds total

3 pounds veal neck bones, cut into 2-inch pieces

2 tablespoons olive oil

1 large onion, minced

2 cans (35 ounces each) tomatoes, pureed with their
    liquid

$2\frac{1}{2}$ cups water

3 cups canned tomato sauce

1 can (6 ounces) tomato paste

3 large cloves garlic, peeled

2 teaspoons dried basil, crumbled

1 tablespoon sugar

1 teaspoon red pepper flakes

Salt to taste

$1\frac{1}{2}$ pounds spaghetti or tubular pasta

Freshly grated Locatelli to taste

In a casserole, combine the lamb and veal with enough cold water to cover the meat by 2 inches. Bring the liquid to a boil and simmer for 10 minutes. Remove the meat, drain, and pat dry.

In the casserole, heat the oil over moderate heat until hot. Add the onion and cook it, stirring occasionally, until golden. Return the meat to the casserole and add the tomatoes, water, tomato sauce, tomato paste, garlic, basil, sugar, pepper flakes, and salt. Bring to a boil, and simmer, partially covered, stirring occasionally, for 2 to $2\frac{1}{2}$ hours, or until the meat is tender.

Cook the pasta according to package directions and drain. Transfer it to a large bowl, add enough sauce to coat, and toss to combine. Sprinkle with cheese. Transfer the meat to a platter and spoon some sauce over it. Serve the meat and pasta separately with a mixed green salad (recipe on page 25).

Serves 6 to 8   Recipe Catherine Scorsese

Elizabeth Street, 1996. Charles Scorsese grew up in 241, the building
with the striped awning, across the street from Catherine, who lived in
232. They raised their sons up the street, in 253.

STUFFED MEAT LOAF

¼ cup fresh bread crumbs

½ cup milk

1 small onion, minced

1 tablespoon olive oil

8 ounces each ground pork, veal, and beef

¼ cup freshly grated Locatelli or Parmesan

1 large egg, lightly beaten

1 cup tomato sauce

2 tablespoons minced fresh parsley leaves

Salt and pepper to taste

2 to 3 slices salami

3 hard-cooked eggs, halved

2 to 3 slices provolone

2 to 3 slices ham

½ cup ketchup diluted with ¼ cup water

Bread crumbs to taste

Preheat the oven to 350 degrees F.

In a large bowl, soak the bread crumbs in the milk until soft.

In a small skillet set over moderate heat, cook the onion in the oil, stirring, until softened. Transfer to the bowl. Add the meat, grated cheese, egg, tomato sauce, parsley, and salt and pepper, and gently mix to combine.

In an oiled baking dish, arrange half the meat, patting it down into a flattened loaf shape. Arrange enough of the salami over the meat to cover it completely, add a row of egg halves down the center, and cover with a layer of the provolone and ham. Top with the remaining ground meat, forming the mixture into a loaf. Pour the ketchup mixture over the loaf and sprinkle with the bread crumbs. Bake for 1 hour, covered with foil. Remove the cover and bake for 30 minutes more, basting with the pan juices. Let stand for 15 minutes before slicing.

Serves 4 to 6   Recipe Fanny di Giovanni

Catherine Scorsese

MARY ALBANESE

GEORGIA DOWNARD: Did you buy the chicken from the butcher on Elizabeth Street?

CATHERINE SCORSESE: I bought the chicken from Mary. It was a butcher shop, but she had one section of the store, it was all chickens. She had good chickens. We used to have a lot of fun. We'd sit with her outside in the summertime.

GEORGIA DOWNARD: Did she always have the butcher shop there?

CATHERINE SCORSESE: No, it belonged to her husband. Then he, by mistake, he was shot and killed. And Mary remained without her husband. She had two little boys. So the boys grew up without a father. But everybody used to go to her for meat. She was such a sweet honey. And that was such a tragedy that happened. They were only married, I think, not even a year. It was a mistake—they were out to hit one person but they got the wrong man. That was so sad.

GEORGIA DOWNARD: She must have worked very hard.

CATHERINE SCORSESE: She did. She used to do all of the cutting of the meat. Her son used to clean it off and prepare it for her. And everybody knew Mary. Everybody. The shop was always full of people, whether they bought anything or not. They all loved her.

GEORGIA DOWNARD: It's very unusual to see a woman doing that work.

CATHERINE SCORSESE: Of course the men would help her carry the big animals, you know. Because they would have to take them apart.

Mary Albanese, now 94: "They ask me when I'm going to retire. When these eyes close, I'll go on vacation."

Stewed Chicken

6 whole chicken legs, separated into drumsticks and
    thighs
½ cup olive oil
6 large onions, sliced
6 potatoes, peeled and quartered
3 carrots, peeled and sliced
1 large can sliced mushrooms
2 cups chicken broth
1 cup water
Salt and pepper to taste
2 tablespoons cornstarch
A few drops Gravy Master, or to taste, for color

Remove the skin from the chicken. Rinse and pat dry.

In a large skillet set over moderately high heat, heat ¼ cup of
the oil until hot. Add the chicken in batches and cook until
brown on both sides—about 6 to 8 minutes. When the
chicken is browned, transfer it to a platter.

Add 2 tablespoons oil to the skillet and heat it over moderate heat until hot. Add the onions and cook, stirring frequently, until softened—about 5 minutes. Transfer the onions to a plate.

Add the remaining oil to the skillet and heat it over moderate heat until hot. Add the potatoes and cook them, turning occasionally, until golden brown.

In a casserole, combine the chicken, onions, and potatoes. Add the carrots, mushrooms, broth, water, and salt and pepper. Bring to a boil, then reduce heat and simmer, covered, for 30 minutes, or until the chicken is tender.

In a small bowl, combine the cornstarch with $\frac{1}{2}$ cup of the cooking liquid and Gravy Master. Add to the simmering liquid in a stream, stirring, and simmer until slightly thickened.

Serves 6   Recipe Catherine Scorsese

PASTA

GEORGIA DOWNARD: Did you cook pasta when your sons were growing up?

CATHERINE SCORSESE: I used to cook pasta almost every night. They loved it. I used to buy fresh macaroni on Grand Street, spaghetti, whatever was fresh. I didn't make my own dough.

My son Frank does now, because he's got machines. I wouldn't believe him at first so he said to me, "Come for dinner tonight." And it was delicious.

CAVATELLI WITH BROCCOLI

3 tablespoons olive oil
4 cloves garlic, minced
1 head broccoli, cut into florets
2 cups chicken broth
Salt to taste
Cayenne pepper or red pepper flakes to taste
1 pound cavatelli
Freshly grated Locatelli or Parmesan

In a large saucepan set over moderate heat, heat the oil until hot, add the garlic, and cook, stirring, for 1 minute. Add the broccoli and toss to coat with the oil. Add the chicken broth and salt and cayenne and bring the liquid to a boil. Simmer for 6 to 8 minutes, or until the broccoli is tender.

Meanwhile, in a large saucepan of boiling salted water, cook the cavatelli until barely tender. Drain and add to the broccoli mixture. Simmer until tender. Serve with the cheese.

Serves 4   Recipe Catherine Scorsese

LASAGNE WITH MEAT SAUCE

2 pounds ricotta cheese

1 large egg, lightly beaten

¾ cup freshly grated Locatelli or Parmesan

2 tablespoons minced fresh parsley

½ recipe Tomato Sauce with Meat (recipe on page 7)

Olive oil

16 lasagne noodles

1 pound mozzarella, sliced thin

Preheat the oven to 350 degrees F.

In a bowl, combine the ricotta, egg, ¼ cup of the grated cheese, parsley, and 1 cup of the Tomato Sauce with Meat.

To a large pan of boiling salted water, add the oil and lasagne noodles and cook until barely tender. Drain, rinse under cold water, and drain again.

Into a large rectangular baking dish, ladle enough sauce to cover the bottom. Cover with 4 noodles and top with a layer of the ricotta mixture, mozzarella, some sauce, and ¼ cup of the grated cheese. Make 3 more layers. Cover with foil and bake for 1 hour. Remove the foil and bake for 30 minutes more. Let stand for 10 minutes before serving.

Serves 8   Recipe Catherine Scorsese

CHILDREN'S LUNCH

I made sandwiches for my kids in the morning, and I used to cut them up. We used to just put them in little bags, the nice heavy bags, so the food didn't go through. And that was it because I couldn't stay at home all day. At three o'clock I used to pick Martin up, because he was a little younger than Frankie. And we used to walk around. We had friends, we were all friends in the neighborhood. We would do our grocery shopping on the way home—everything was at our disposal. All of the stores were just lined up. I used to go to Di Palo's on Mott Street, though, to buy the cold cuts and cheese because they had the best.

On Saturdays we always had Jewish delicatessen food. But on Sundays we had pasta and sauce. That was the tradition.

Catherine Scorsese

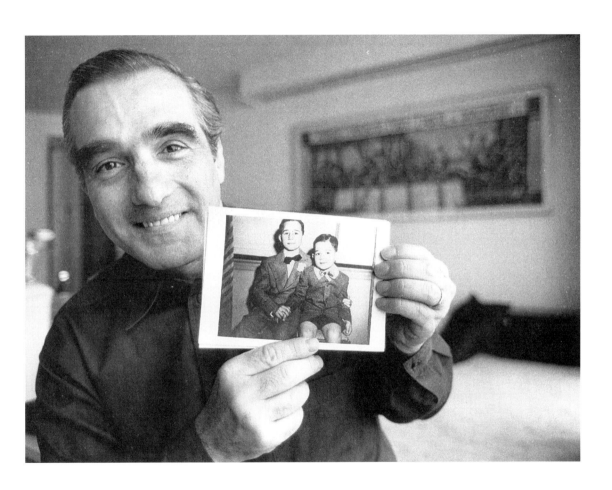

Martin Scorsese with a photograph of himself and his older brother, Frank, as children.

SICILIAN PRONUNCIATION

FANNY DI GIOVANNI: Katie, tell Georgia how we make fun when we go down to Di Palo's and people ask for capicole.

CATHERINE SCORSESE: It's capicole, but they say "capicoli." I can't stand it when they say "mozzarella." "Mozzarella" is English. "Moozarella" is Italian.

GEORGIA DOWNARD: How do you say "ricotta"?

CATHERINE SCORSESE: "Rigotta."

GEORGIA DOWNARD: And you say "putensa" instead of "puttanesca," and "manacotti," right?

CATHERINE SCORSESE: "Manicotti," that's the limit. When we used to go to Di Palo's, we'd stand there and laugh.

Di Palo's, 1996.

PASTA PUTENSA

¼ cup olive oil

1 cup minced onion

1 can (2 ounces) anchovies, drained, oil reserved, chopped

2 tablespoons minced garlic

1 can (35 ounces) Italian plum tomatoes, including liquid, chopped fine

1 bottle (3 ounces) capers, drained and plumped in water for 10 minutes

12 oil-cured olives, pitted and halved

¼ to ½ teaspoon red pepper flakes, or to taste

2 tablespoons minced fresh basil or 1 teaspoon dried, crumbled

Salt to taste

1 pound linguini

Freshly grated Locatelli or Parmesan

In a large saucepan set over moderate heat, heat the oil until hot. Add the onion and cook, stirring, for 3 minutes, or until translucent. Pour off the oil and add the anchovies, their oil, and the garlic to the pan. Cook, stirring, for 2 minutes more. Add the tomatoes, capers, olives, pepper flakes, basil, and salt. Bring the mixture to a boil, reduce heat, and simmer, covered, stirring occasionally, for 45 minutes.

Meanwhile, in a large saucepan of boiling salted water, cook the linguini until al dente, drain, and transfer it to a large bowl. Add the sauce and toss to combine. Serve with the cheese.

Serves 4 to 6   Recipe Teresa Scorsese

POTATO FRITTATA

2 large red potatoes, peeled and cut into 1-inch wedges
about ⅛-inch thick
1 cup sliced onion
4 to 5 tablespoons olive oil, or to taste
Salt and freshly ground black pepper to taste
4 large eggs
2 to 3 tablespoons freshly grated Parmesan
Minced fresh parsley leaves

Pat dry the potatoes and onions.

In a large, nonstick skillet set over moderate heat, heat 2
tablespoons of the oil until hot. Add the potatoes, onions,
and salt and pepper and fry the vegetables, stirring occasionally, until golden brown and just tender. Transfer to a plate.

In a bowl, combine the eggs, Parmesan, and salt and pepper.
Add the vegetable mixture and gently stir to combine.

Catherine Scorsese

Potato Frittata.

Add 1 to 2 tablespoons of oil to the skillet and heat it over moderate heat until hot. Add the vegetable and egg mixture and cook it over moderately low heat until golden brown and set on the underside. Invert a plate over the skillet and flip the frittata onto the plate.

Add another tablespoon of oil to the skillet and slide the frittata back in, uncooked side down. Cook until completely set.

Transfer to a plate and cut into wedges. Sprinkle with parsley.

Serves 4 to 6   Recipe Domenica Cappa

KATIE'S TIP

Use a heavy frying pan, not too big (a 9-inch skillet is good), and don't put too much oil in it. Just enough so the frittata are golden brown. If you burn them, you'd have to give them to the cat. Only he would refuse them too!

SERVING TIP

Frittata was made with potatoes and eggs—and also with vegetables, like zucchini, asparagus, and broccoli—and was cut like a pie. And then they also used to put it in Italian bread. We used to buy little rolls in the store, they were pointed rolls. They were so delicious.

My mother used to make sandwiches and then she used to put them in a warm towel and wrap them up. She had to put the eggs on top of the potatoes, because some of my brothers didn't want the eggs so they ate it plain. That's what we had when we went to school.

STUFFED SQUID WITH TOMATO SAUCE

For the sauce :
1 cup minced onion
4 cloves garlic, minced
2 tablespoons olive oil
2 cans (28 ounces each) crushed tomatoes in puree
1 cup water
1 can (15 ounces) tomato sauce
2 carrots, peeled and cut into 2-inch lengths
1 boiling potato, peeled and left whole
1 teaspoon dried basil, crumbled
Cayenne pepper to taste
Salt to taste

3 pounds squid, cleaned
1 small onion, minced fine
2 cloves garlic, minced fine
2 tablespoons olive oil

½ **pound sea legs, diced small**
2 **hard-cooked eggs, finely chopped**
½ **cup fresh bread crumbs**
⅓ **cup freshly grated Locatelli or Parmesan**
Salt and pepper to taste
1 **pound linguini**
Freshly grated Locatelli or Parmesan to taste

Make the sauce: In a casserole set over moderate heat, cook the onion and garlic in the oil, stirring occasionally, for 5 minutes, or until translucent. In a blender or food processor, puree the tomatoes, water, and tomato sauce until smooth and add it to the casserole. Add the carrots, potato, basil, cayenne, and salt. Bring the liquid to a boil and simmer, partially covered, stirring occasionally, for 1 hour.

Rinse the squid and turn the body sacs inside out. Mince the tentacles.

In a skillet set over moderate heat, cook the onion and garlic in the oil, stirring occasionally, for 2 minutes. Add the squid tentacles and cook, stirring occasionally, for 3 minutes more.

Transfer to a bowl. Add the sea legs, eggs, bread crumbs, grated cheese, and salt and pepper. Combine the mixture well.

Stuff the squid with the bread-crumb mixture and close with a toothpick. Add the squid to the sauce and simmer for 10 to 15 minutes, or until just tender. Transfer the squid to a serving dish.

Meanwhile, cook the linguini according to package directions, drain, and transfer it to a large bowl. Add enough sauce to coat the pasta and toss to combine. Sprinkle with cheese. Serve the squid separately with a mixed green salad (recipe page 25).

Serves 6 to 8   Recipe Catherine Scorsese

Catherine, Charles with Martin on his lap, and Catherine's
brother Andrew Cappa.

Ricotta Pie

For the crust:

2 cups all-purpose flour

1 tablespoon sugar

1 teaspoon baking powder

$\frac{1}{4}$ teaspoon salt

$\frac{1}{2}$ cup cold vegetable shortening, cut into bits

1 large egg, beaten lightly

2 to 3 tablespoons ice water

$1\frac{1}{2}$ pounds ricotta, drained well

$\frac{3}{4}$ cup sugar

5 large eggs

1 tablespoon vanilla extract

$\frac{1}{2}$ teaspoon cinnamon

$\frac{1}{2}$ cup diced candied fruit

$\frac{1}{2}$ cup semisweet chocolate chips

Make the pie crust :Into a bowl, sift the flour, sugar, baking powder, and salt. Add the shortening and blend until the mixture resembles coarse crumbs. In a bowl, whisk together the egg and 2 tablespoons of the ice water. Add the egg mixture to the flour mixture and toss to combine, adding more water if necessary to form a dough. Chill the dough, wrapped in plastic, until firm.

On a lightly floured surface, roll out the dough into a circle ⅛ inch thick and fit it into a 9-inch pie pan. Crimp the edge, prick the bottom, and chill while making the filling.

Preheat the oven to 350 degrees F. In a large bowl with an electric mixer, beat the ricotta with the sugar until smooth. Add the eggs, one at a time, beating well after each addition. Beat in the vanilla and cinnamon. Stir in the candied fruit and chocolate chips. Pour the filling into the pie shell.

Bake the pie for 45 minutes, or until just set. Let cool and chill.

Makes one 9-inch pie   Recipe Teresa Scorsese

SAINT LUCY'S DAY

CATHERINE SCORSESE: Saint Lucy (Santa Lucia) was the patron saint for eyes. So Charlie used to wear glasses and he said to me one day: "I'm going to go have a pair of glasses made." I said: "What for? You've got glasses." He said: "These are different. When I come back, I'll show you." It was that he didn't want to wear glasses anymore.

Saint Lucy had these beautiful eyes and all of the men came after her because she was a virgin. So not to commit a mortal sin, she plucked her eyes out. God loved her so much that he made her eyes grow back. And so she's always pictured holding a plate with two human eyes on it.

On Saint Lucy's Day (December 13), you can't eat anything baked with wheat. The food made for that day is panelle, little rectangular pancakes made with chickpea paste and you find this kind of recipe going back to Ancient Rome. They'd give it out in carts on the streets. The taste is extraordinary and the design of it is quite beautiful. [Panelle sometimes have a pressed design on top.] Also orangina, which is fried rice balls. Inside the rice ball is a small core of red sauce, peas, and meat. These are only made in Brooklyn today. They are simple to make, but it is hard to keep the center together with the rice, and the rice has a creamy quality to it.

My husband made a prayer to Saint Lucy. He asked her if she would let him remove his glasses forever, he would never eat bread on that day again. Do you know that he removed his glasses, and he saw better. Isn't that amazing? I'm telling you he was so happy. And we made the pasta and ate it.

S. LUCIA

PANELLE

(Deep-Fried Chickpea Cakes)

3 cups cold water
1½ teaspoons salt, or to taste
½ pound (2 cups) chickpea (ceci) flour (available at
    specialty food stores), sifted
3 tablespoons freshly grated Locatelli or Parmesan
2 tablespoons minced fresh parsley
Vegetable oil for deep frying

In a saucepan, mix the water and salt and stir until salt is
dissolved. Gradually add the flour, whisking until mixture
is smooth. Set the saucepan over medium-low heat and
cook, stirring continually, until mixture comes away from
sides of pan, about 10 to 15 minutes. Stir in cheese and
parsley and transfer mixture to an oiled jelly-roll pan or
baking sheet, spreading it into an even layer about
½ inch thick. Let cool. (Mixture may be chilled, covered,

for several hours or overnight.) Cut the panelle into squares, rectangles, or circles about 3 inches in diameter.

In a deep-fat fryer or heavy saucepan, heat the oil until it reaches 365 degrees F. Add the panelle in batches and fry until golden brown, about 3 to 5 minutes. Drain on paper towels and serve while still hot.

Serves 4, makes twelve 3-inch squares

SERVING TIP

The dough—very similar in preparation to polenta— when cooled can be cut into a variety of shapes. Panelle make wonderful hors d'oeuvres.

THE MOVIES:
COOKING ON THE SET

―――――

"From my very first short films, we had scenes
with cooking in them." MARTIN SCORSESE

GOODFELLAS (1990)

DAVID LETTERMAN: Has there ever been a scene in a film that you've done, where you just turned your back on it and crossed your fingers and said, "I don't have a clue here," and just winged it?

MARTIN SCORSESE: For example, the scene I did with my mother in *GoodFellas.* I had a clue, but I had no idea what she was going to say. So we put two cameras in a very small dining room in Queens.

DAVID LETTERMAN: This is after the boys have come back from a grisly mission . . .

MARTIN SCORSESE: Yes, they had an unfortunate incident, and it was in the trunk. We didn't tell her there was a body in the trunk. So they come in the middle of the night, and she says, Come, sit down, and have some food, and that sort of thing. So I put a wide shot on my mother, Joe Pesci, Ray Liotta, Bob De Niro and a tighter one on Joe Pesci and my mother—two cameras simultaneously. She started to talk.

Catherine Scorsese

We said, "Don't talk. Save it," and we started rolling. There was only one written line in that scene. Everything else she winged.

DAVID LETTERMAN: Is it true that for that scene and others she actually cooked the food?

MARTIN SCORSESE: Yes, for that scene she made a snack: potatoes and eggs, lots of bread, and pizza.

DAVID LETTERMAN: She cooks for film scenes and also for the crew and has for a very long time?

MARTIN SCORSESE: It's very important. From my very first short films, we had scenes with cooking in them. In *GoodFellas*, the food was very important, the menu was important. She supervised the different dishes that were in the picture and actually cooked the food.

(Late Night with David Letterman, NBC, 1991)

CAST

Tommy's mother: Catherine Scorsese
Tommy: Joe Pesci
Jimmy: Robert De Niro
Henry: Ray Liotta

Interior. The kitchen in Tommy's mother's house. The light comes on, and Tommy's mother appears in her housecoat.

TOMMY'S MOTHER: Hey, look who's here. Look who's here.

TOMMY: Hey, Ma, what are you doing up?

TOMMY'S MOTHER: What are you doing? *(She sees blood on him.)* What happened? What—

TOMMY: No, no, nothing. I hit, I hit, I hit something on the road.

TOMMY'S MOTHER: What happened to you?

TOMMY: Jimmy will tell you.

TOMMY'S MOTHER: What happened? What happened to him?

JIMMY: Nothing, nothing, nothing, nothing. How are you, sweetheart?

TOMMY'S MOTHER: What happened, boys?

JIMMY: How are you, sweetheart?

TOMMY'S MOTHER: Ah, Jim. We haven't seen you in so long!

Ray Liotta, Joe Pesci, Catherine Scorsese, and Robert De Niro in *GoodFellas*.

What happened to him? I hate to see him that way.
And you too.

HENRY: Hi, how are you?

TOMMY'S MOTHER: How are you?

HENRY: Good.

TOMMY'S MOTHER: But what happened? Tell me what happened.

JIMMY: What are you doing up so late?

TOMMY'S MOTHER: Well, he came in. Youse came in. I figured, you know . . . I'm, I'm so happy to see him.

JIMMY: Do you know what time it is?

TOMMY'S MOTHER: Look, go inside. Make yourselves comfortable. I'll make you something to eat.

JIMMY: No.

HENRY: No. No, no, no, no, no, no.

JIMMY: No, no, no. Go to sleep. Go to sleep. We're gonna leave. We're just getting the shovel, we're gonna change and we're gonna go out.

TOMMY'S MOTHER: No, I can't sleep. Not while he's home. No. I haven't seen him so long.

JIMMY: No, no.

TOMMY'S MOTHER: I want to see him. Go ahead, youse go inside.

JIMMY: No, but you don't want—

Interior. The dining room in Tommy's mother's house. Later.
Henry, Jimmy, and Tommy are sitting around the kitchen table
eating pasta. Tommy's mother is pleased to have their company.

TOMMY: This stuff is great but it's like lead. Ba boom.

TOMMY'S MOTHER: So tell me, tell me, where have you been? I haven't seen you. I haven't even— You haven't even called or anything. Where have you been?

TOMMY: Ma. Mom, I been working nights.

TOMMY'S MOTHER: And?

TOMMY: And, well, tonight we were out late. We took a ride on the . . . out to the country and we hit one of those deers. That's where all the blood came from. I told you. Jimmy told you before. I went to change.

TOMMY'S MOTHER: And?

TOMMY: Anyway, you know, it reminds me, Ma. I need this knife. I'm gonna take this. It's okay?

TOMMY'S MOTHER: Okay, yeah. Bring it back, though, you know.

TOMMY: I just need it for a little while. Well, the poor thing, you know, he got— I hit him in his, uh— We hit the deer and his paw— What do you call it?

TOMMY'S MOTHER: The paw. The paw. His foot.

TOMMY: The paw, uh . . .

JIMMY: The hoof.

TOMMY: The hoof got caught in that grille. I got to, I got to hack it off.

TOMMY'S MOTHER: Ooh!

TOMMY: M-M-Ma, it's a sin. You gonna leave it there, you know? So anyway, I'll, I'll bring your knife back after . . . Anyway . . .

JIMMY: Delicious. Delicious.

TOMMY'S MOTHER: Thank you. *(To Tommy.)* Why don't you get yourself a nice girl?

TOMMY: I get a nice one almost every night, Ma.

TOMMY'S MOTHER: Yeah, but get yourself a girl so you can settle down. That's what I mean.

TOMMY: I settle down almost every night, but then in the morning I'm free. I love you! I wanna be wi− *(He kisses her.)* I wanna be with you!

(Martin Scorsese and Nicholas Pileggi: *GoodFellas*)

POACHED EGGS WITH PEAS

1 cup minced onion
2 tablespoons olive oil
1 can (15½ ounces) Le Sueur peas, including liquid
Salt and pepper to taste
2 large eggs

In a saucepan set over moderate heat, cook the onion in the oil, stirring occasionally, for 5 minutes, or until translucent. Add the peas and liquid, salt and pepper and simmer, covered, for 5 minutes.

Crack the eggs into a small bowl and carefully lower them into the simmering liquid. Gently simmer, basting with the cooking juices, until the eggs are cooked to the desired doneness.

Serves 1   Recipe Catherine Scorsese

MEATBALLS

CATHERINE SCORSESE: My husband, Charlie, was playing Vinnie, one of the gangsters [in *GoodFellas*]. He'd come home and I'd say, "So, Charlie, what did you do today?" And he'd say, "Well, today they killed so-and-so." And the next day he'd come home and I'd say, "Well, what did you do today?" And he'd say, "Well, they dumped the bodies today." Day after day after day. I said, "Marty, what's going on? What's this movie about? Only killing?" He said, "Ma, it's the book. It's the way it is." I played the mother of Tommy, and he's always killing, too.

I made sixty meatballs for Charlie to take for his scene. In my scene, Tommy brings his friends home and his mother cooks for them. I play his mother, so I said to Marty, "What am I going to make for them?" And he said, "Make pasta and beans, just like you used to make for me—or eggs." If he'd come home late from a date or from being over at NYU, I'd get up and make him something to eat, and then I'd go back to sleep. And, you know, it was in the middle of the night, so I'd make him something like eggs or pasta and beans. He said, "If it was good enough for me, it's good enough for them."

(Mary Pat Kelly: *Martin Scorsese: A Journey*)

Catherine Scorsese

CHICKEN ESCAROLE SOUP
WITH TINY MEATBALLS

6 whole chicken legs

Salt to taste

2 cups chicken stock or broth

2 carrots, peeled and halved

1 large onion, peeled and halved

3 celery stalks, strings removed

2 cloves garlic, peeled

2 large plum tomatoes, peeled, seeded, and chopped

Freshly ground black pepper to taste

1 large head escarole ($1\frac{3}{4}$ pounds), trimmed and
    washed well

For the meatballs:

6 ounces each ground pork, veal, and beef

1 large egg

$\frac{1}{2}$ to $\frac{2}{3}$ cup milk

1 teaspoon dried basil, crumbled

$\frac{1}{4}$ **cup freshly grated Parmesan**
1 tablespoon minced fresh parsley
2 teaspoons garlic powder
Salt and pepper to taste

Freshly grated Parmesan

Remove the skin and all the fat from the chicken, transfer to a bowl, cover with cold water and salt, and let soak for 15 minutes. Drain.

In a casserole, combine the chicken, stock, carrots, onion, celery, garlic, tomatoes, and salt and pepper with enough water to cover. Bring to a boil, then reduce heat and simmer, partially covered, skimming frequently, for $1\frac{1}{2}$ hours.

Meanwhile, in a large saucepan of boiling water, cook the escarole for 3 to 5 minutes, or until tender. Drain, let cool, and chop.

Make the meatballs: In a bowl, combine all the ingredients and form into 1-inch balls. Chill them until ready to cook.

Catherine Scorsese

Strain the soup into a clean saucepan, reserving the chicken and vegetables. Skim the surface of fat. Remove the chicken from the bones and dice. Slice the vegetables and return the vegetables and chicken to the pan.

Bring the soup to a simmer, add the escarole and meatballs, and simmer, covered, for 30 minutes. Ladle into soup bowls and sprinkle with Parmesan.

Serves 6   Recipe Teresa Scorsese

KATIE'S TIP

When making these raw little meatballs, to make them small and solid, you have to have enough stuffing and meat to roll them. You put it between your two palms and roll. The more you roll, the rounder it gets.

JOE PESCI

REGIS PHILBIN *(as Catherine cooks):* You never knew how much of each ingredient to put in, you just knew by touch.

CATHERINE SCORSESE: My mother used to cook like that. All the old folks cooked like that. They never used measurements. If it came good, it came good. If it didn't, too bad. Now I'm going to use my hands, because hands were made before forks.

REGIS PHILBIN: That scene in *GoodFellas*—the one where Joe Pesci comes home after murdering this guy, sat down and said: "What's for dinner, Mom?"—did you actually cook that food?

CATHERINE SCORSESE: Yes. Pasta with kidney beans. Joe kept eating and his stomach got like a balloon.

JOE PESCI: Marty said to me before the scene: "What do you want to eat?" I ordered pasta with kidney beans and eggplant Parmesan. Marty said don't eat a lot because we'll have to do this scene a lot of times. I said, "I don't care. I'm going to keep eating."

(*Live with Regis and Kathie Lee*, ABC, 1993)

Catherine Scorsese and Joe Pesci in *GoodFellas*.

PASTA E FAGIOLI

(Pasta and Bean Soup)

1 cup minced onion
2 tablespoons olive oil
1 can (16 ounces) whole tomatoes, including
    liquid
6 cups water
2 cans (13 ounces each) cannellini beans, drained
1 tablespoon tomato paste
Salt and pepper to taste
12 ounces medium pasta shells
Freshly grated Parmesan

In a large saucepan set over moderate heat, cook the onion in the oil, stirring occasionally, for 5 minutes. Drain the tomatoes, reserving the liquid, and coarsely chop. Add the tomatoes, reserved liquid, water, beans, tomato paste, and salt and pepper to the pan. Bring to a boil and simmer, stirring occasionally, for 20 minutes. Add 2 more cups of water and simmer for 10 minutes more.

Catherine Scorsese

Meanwhile, in a large pan of boiling salted water, cook the pasta until barely tender. Drain. Add the pasta to the soup and, if necessary, add enough water to just cover. Simmer until heated through. Let stand for 5 minutes before serving. Serve with the Parmesan.

Serves 6   Recipe Catherine Scorsese

COOKING TIP

It's delicious if you fry it the next day. Also, the pasta with peas (recipe on page 128) is good this way. You add a bit of olive oil and stir-fry it.

EGGPLANT PARMIGIANA

**2 eggplants, peeled and cut lengthwise into ¼-inch
slices**
Salt to taste
2 cups dry bread crumbs
Pepper to taste
1 cup freshly grated Locatelli
**2 tablespoons minced fresh basil (or 2 teaspoons dried
basil)**
3 large eggs
1 cup milk
3 to 4 cups Tomato Sauce (see recipe on page 90)
¾ cup olive oil, or to taste
1 pound mozzarella, sliced thin

Sprinkle the eggplant slices with salt to taste, arrange in a
colander, and cover with a plate or shallow bowl. Top with
weight (such as a gallon can of oil) and let drain, 20 minutes. Rinse off excess salt and pat dry with paper towels.

Preheat the oven to 350 degrees F.

In a shallow bowl, combine the bread crumbs, salt and pepper to taste, half the Locatelli, the basil, and the parsley.

In another shallow bowl, whisk together the eggs and milk.

Dip the eggplant in the egg-milk mixture, letting the excess drip off, and dredge in the bread-crumb mixture.

In a large skillet set over moderate heat, heat 3 to 4 tablespoons of olive oil until hot. Add enough eggplant slices to fry in one layer and cook for 2 to 3 minutes on each side, or until golden brown. Transfer to a platter lined with paper towels to drain. Continue cooking the remaining eggplant, adding oil as necessary, until all is browned.

Into an oiled 9-by-13-inch shallow baking dish, spoon a layer of tomato sauce. Arrange in layers the eggplant, mozzarella, a sprinkling of Locatelli, and more sauce.

Bake in the oven, covered with foil, for 15 minutes. Remove foil and bake for 15 minutes more, or until cheese is melted and sauce is bubbling.

Serves 6   Recipe Catherine Scorsese

ROBERT DE NIRO

DAVID LETTERMAN: Do you enjoy being in Martin's films?

CATHERINE SCORSESE: I have to be in the films, otherwise he threatens me.

DAVID LETTERMAN *(watching Catherine prepare pizza)*: Robert De Niro comes over, and you make this pizza.

CATHERINE SCORSESE: Robert De Niro loves it. He says I make the best pizza in the world.

DAVID LETTERMAN: Why is this different from other pizza?

CATHERINE SCORSESE: Because it's made by me.

DAVID LETTERMAN: What sort of table manners does Robert De Niro have? Does he eat in his T-shirt?

CATHERINE SCORSESE: No! He comes dressed up in clothes. What's the matter with you? *(She slices the pizza.)*

Robert De Niro and Catherine Scorsese.

DAVID LETTERMAN: Yes, what *is* wrong with me? *(The audience laughs.)*

You're using scissors!

CATHERINE SCORSESE: My mother-in-law taught me to use scissors. You cut better with them and don't scratch the pan.

(Late Night with David Letterman)

Catherine Scorsese

TOMATO AND CHEESE PIZZA

For the sauce:

1½ cups minced onion

3 tablespoons olive oil

2 cans (28 ounces each) whole tomatoes, including
     liquid, coarsely chopped

1 can (15 ounces) tomato sauce

1 teaspoon dried basil, crumbled

Salt to taste

Cayenne pepper to taste

Sugar to taste

1 pound pizza dough, thawed according to package
     directions if frozen

2 cups grated mozzarella

¼ to ⅓ cup freshly grated Locatelli or Parmesan

Make the sauce: In a large saucepan set over moderate
heat, cook the onion in the oil, stirring occasionally, for 5

Katie's Pizza.

minutes. Add the tomatoes, tomato sauce, basil, salt, cayenne, and sugar. Bring to a boil and simmer, covered, stirring occasionally, for 30 minutes.

Preheat the oven to 400 degrees F. Pat the dough into an oiled jelly-roll pan, sprinkle with the mozzarella, spreading it in an even layer, and top with enough sauce to coat. (The sauce should be chunky.) Sprinkle with cheese. Bake for 20 minutes, or until the crust is golden brown.

Makes 1 pizza, serving 4 to 6

VARIATIONS

Sausage Pizza : Same as above except after the mozzarella add $\frac{1}{2}$ pound cooked sliced sausage.
Pepperoni Pizza : Same as above except after the mozzarella add $\frac{1}{2}$ pound thinly sliced pepperoni.

A MOTHER'S CARE

In *It's Not Just You, Murray!* (Martin Scorsese's second student film), Catherine Scorsese plays the mother who is constantly offering her son a plate of spaghetti.

"There were a lot of times when he was working at NYU when I used to get into a cab and bring him some food and then wait to make sure he ate it. I used to say to him: 'Look, Marty, don't worry. It'll all come out in the wash.' "

Catherine Scorsese in *It's Not Just You, Murray!*, 1964.

PASTA WITH PEAS
AND SAUSAGE

1 cup minced onion

2 tablespoons olive oil

1 pound sweet Italian sausage, removed from
     casing

2 cups tomato sauce

2 cans (15½ ounces each) Le Sueur peas, including
     liquid

1½ cups water

Salt and pepper to taste

1 teaspoon dried basil, crumbled

1 pound elbow macaroni

Freshly grated Parmesan

Catherine Scorsese

In a large saucepan set over moderate heat, cook the onion in the oil, stirring occasionally, for 5 minutes. Add the sausage and cook it until no longer pink. Drain, then add the tomato sauce, peas and liquid, water, salt and pepper, and basil. Bring to a boil and simmer for 20 minutes.

Meanwhile, in a large saucepan of boiling salted water, cook the macaroni until barely tender, drain, and add to the sauce. Simmer until heated through. Let stand for 5 minutes before serving. Serve with the Parmesan.

Serves 4 to 6   Recipe Catherine Scorsese

Pork-Filled Calzone

Catherine prepares this dish in Who's That Knocking at My Door?*, 1969. It is served on the Feast of the Immaculate Conception.*

1 pound pizza dough, thawed according to package directions if frozen

1 pound ground pork
1 teaspoon salt
White pepper to taste
Egg glaze made by beating 1 large egg with 1 teaspoon water and a pinch of salt

Preheat the oven to 350 degrees F.

On a lightly floured surface, roll out the dough into a circle about $\frac{1}{8}$ inch thick.

In a bowl, combine the pork, salt, and pepper. Arrange the pork over half the dough, leaving a 1-inch border. Brush the edge of the dough with water and fold the dough over the filling. Crimp the edge to seal.

Transfer the dough to an oiled baking sheet and brush with the glaze. Bake for 45 minutes, or until juices run clear.

Serves 6   Recipe Catherine Scorsese

LENTIL SOUP

"Charlie loved this. It would be a whole meal. They all loved it. As for me, I didn't care for it at all."

1 pound lentils
1½ cups sliced carrot
1½ cups finely chopped onion
1 cup sliced celery
3 tablespoons olive oil
4 cups beef stock or broth
2 cups water
Salt and pepper to taste

Catherine Scorsese

In a bowl, combine the lentils with enough water to cover by 2 inches and let soak for 1 hour. Drain.

In a casserole set over moderate heat, cook the carrot, onion, and celery in the oil, stirring occasionally, for 5 minutes. Add the lentils, stock, water, and salt and pepper. Bring to a boil, then reduce heat and simmer, covered, for 40 to 45 minutes, or until the lentils are tender.

Serves 10 to 12   Recipe Teresa Scorsese

Martin Scorsese, Robert De Niro, and Catherine Scorsese on the set of *Taxi Driver*, **1976. (This scene was eventually dropped.)**

Charles, Catherine, and Martin Scorsese with Aunt Dora (Charles's sister-in-law) on the set of
New York, New York, 1977. Charles is wearing a suit of Edward G. Robinson's from the MGM wardrobe.

Stuffed Leg of Lamb

This is served at Easter.

A 6-pound boned leg of lamb
Salt and freshly ground black pepper to taste
¾ cup fresh bread crumbs
¼ cup olive oil
3 tablespoons minced garlic
½ cup freshly grated Locatelli
3 tablespoons minced fresh parsley leaves

Preheat the oven to 375 degrees F. Pat dry the lamb and season it with salt and pepper.

In a skillet set over moderate heat, cook the bread crumbs in the oil until golden brown, transfer to a bowl, and add the garlic, cheese, parsley, and salt and pepper.

Spread the bread-crumb mixture on the cut side of the lamb, roll to enclose, and tie with string.

Arrange the lamb on a rack in a baking pan, add about 1 inch of water to the pan, and roast for 1 to 1½ hours, or until the meat is medium rare. Let it stand for 10 minutes before carving.

Serves 10 to 12   Recipe Teresa Scorsese

BAKED POTATOES WITH CARROTS, SWEET POTATOES, AND ONIONS

4 large Idaho or russet potatoes, peeled and cut into
    1-inch pieces
2 sweet potatoes, peeled and cut into 1-inch pieces
3 large carrots, peeled, halved lengthwise, and cut into
    $\frac{1}{2}$-inch-thick slices
1 large yellow onion, peeled and cut into 1-inch pieces
1 green bell pepper, diced
$\frac{1}{4}$ cup olive oil
Salt and freshly ground black pepper to taste

Preheat the oven to 375 degrees F.

In a large bowl, combine all the ingredients and toss to mix well. Transfer to an oiled baking pan and bake, covered with foil, for 30 minutes. Uncover, stir, and bake for an additional 30 to 45 minutes, or until tender.

Place under a preheated broiler about 3 inches from the heat until golden brown.

Serves 6 to 8   Recipe Fanny di Giovanni

RAGING BULL (1980)

CATHERINE SCORSESE: Remember Joey La Motta's wedding? Marty based the scene on our wedding reception. We were married on June 10. And it was so hot that day. We lived on the fourth floor. We were always out on the roof. It used to be beautiful on the roof. Well, we were dying from the heat. I was so hot that when they threw the confetti paper at me, it melted on the wedding gown. That's how hot it was. So we brought the whole party out of the apartment up to the roof. That's why Joey's wedding is on the roof.

CHARLES SCORSESE: Marty was sick the day on *Raging Bull* for the wedding scene, and he said to me, "Go up there and

Italian sausages.

direct it. Tell them what to do up there on the roof." So when I went up there, I saw candelabras, and sliced bread on one side, cold cuts on the other side. I said, "What are these candelabras doing here?" I said, "First, we didn't have candelabras. Secondly, we had rolls made up with ham, cheese, things like that, Swiss cheese—not sliced bread."

Anyway, they took everything off. They took the candelabras off, they went and got rolls—everything. And he had the beer and the soda on the roof, and there was a little confetti on top, which was all right, and cookies. See, at the wedding reception, someone from one end of the roof would holler out, "Hey, Charlie, you want a ham sandwich?" I'd say, "Yeah," and he would throw it over.

(Mary Pat Kelly: *Martin Scorsese: A Journey*)

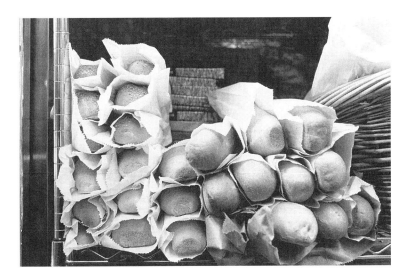

Italian rolls.

VEAL SPIEDINI

For the stuffing:
3 tablespoons olive oil
½ cup minced onion
⅔ cup fresh bread crumbs
2 cloves garlic, minced
¼ cup freshly grated Locatelli
2 tablespoons minced fresh parsley
Salt and pepper
⅓ cup Tomato Sauce (recipe on page 90) or to taste

6 thin slices veal cutlets (about 1 pound)
2 large eggs, beaten lightly
1 cup fresh bread crumbs, seasoned with salt and
    pepper
Olive oil to taste
2 cups Tomato Sauce, or to taste

Preheat the oven to 350 degrees F.

Make the stuffing: In a skillet set over moderate heat, heat the oil until hot. Add the onion and cook, stirring occasionally, until softened. Add the bread crumbs and cook the mixture, stirring occasionally, until golden brown. Add the garlic and cook, stirring, for 1 minute. Transfer the mixture to a bowl and add the cheese, parsley, salt, pepper, and enough tomato sauce to moisten.

Pat dry the veal and season with salt and pepper. Add enough of the bread-crumb mixture to cover each cutlet, spreading it into an even layer. Roll up the veal to enclose the stuffing. Dip each roll in the beaten egg and coat with the crumbs, shaking off the excess. Arrange the rolls, seam side down, in an oiled glass pie plate or baking dish, drizzle with olive oil to taste, and bake in the oven for 30 minutes, or until juices run clear.

Transfer the veal to a serving dish and spoon sauce over the top. Serve with cooked spaghetti and tomato sauce and salad.

Serves 6   Recipe Catherine Scorsese

FRANCIS FORD COPPOLA

I have many happy memories of visiting the Scorsese apartment in Little Italy. Usually it was centered around the table and Mrs. Scorsese's cooking, with Charles in attendance and usually other friends, my brother August as well. I was always very comfortable around Marty's family because more than other Italian Americans, they reminded me of my own family. The conversation was loud, everyone spoke at the same time, and the food was simply great.

My own favorite was Mrs. Scorscsc's Lcmon Chicken, which is on the menu at my Blancaneux Lodge in Belize as just that. Marty makes this very well himself, the trick being, as he puts it, to "drown the chicken in lemon juice." I follow this advice to extremes.

Lemon and Garlic Chicken

3-pound chicken, cut into serving pieces, rinsed and
   patted dry
Scant ½ cup fresh lemon juice
3 tablespoons water
3 tablespoons finely minced garlic
4 tablespoons minced fresh parsley leaves
1 tablespoon olive oil
Salt and freshly ground black pepper to taste

Arrange the chicken in a shallow glass or stainless steel baking dish.

In a small bowl, combine the lemon juice, water, garlic, 2 tablespoons parsley, oil, and salt and pepper. Pour ⅔ of the lemon mixture over the chicken, turning to coat all sides, and let it marinate for 15 minutes.

Preheat the oven to 350 degrees F. Bake the chicken for 20 minutes, basting with the pan juices and adding more of the lemon mixture if the chicken becomes too dry. Turn the chicken and bake, basting with the pan juices, for another 20 minutes, or until the juices run clear.

Arrange the chicken on a broiler pan and place under a pre-heated broiler about 4 inches from the heat until golden brown. Transfer to a serving platter, sprinkle with 1 tablespoon of parsley, and add the remaining tablespoon of parsley to the pan juices. Transfer the pan juices to a sauceboat and serve separately.

Serves 4

Mrs. Scorsese's Lemon Chicken.

THE AGE OF INNOCENCE (1992)

Charles Scorsese had a heart attack during the shooting and died in 1993. This is his last image on film.

KATIE'S REVENGE:

Mrs. Scorsese cleans up the language in *Casino*.

CAST
Artie Piscano: Vinny Vella
Ace: Robert De Niro
Piscano's brother-in-law: George Commando
Piscano's mother: Catherine Scorsese

Interior. San Marino grocery, Kansas City. Piscano and his mother are at the counter of his elderly brother-in-law's store.

PISCANO: They're fightin' over those suitcases [filled with money] again. You know what that means, right? You know what that means, right? That means I gotta take another trip out to Vegas, and it's gonna cost me another couple of grand.

ACE: *(voice-over)* He ran it with his brother-in-law, but mostly what he did was complain, complain about his trips to Vegas, to his brother-in-law and to his mother, all the time.

BROTHER-IN-LAW: *(seated)* You gotta lay down the law. Otherwise, they're gonna make a fool out of you.

PISCANO: They're not gonna make a fool out of me. I write it all down in this book *(holding up a notepad),* every fuckin' nickel that goes down. Right here, receipts . . .

PISCANO'S MOTHER: *(chastising her son)* Hey! Oh!

PISCANO: Oh, sorry—

PISCANO'S MOTHER: What's the matter with you?

PISCANO: Receipts and bills and . . . everything's here.

PISCANO'S MOTHER: Since when do you talk like that?

PISCANO: I'm sorry.

PISCANO'S MOTHER: There's a lot of people here.

PISCANO: Nance gives me trouble and I'll tell him . . . screw around with those suitcases and I'll take the eyes out of his frickin' head.

PISCANO'S MOTHER: Again!

PISCANO: I didn't curse. I said "frickin' head."

PISCANO'S MOTHER: That's enough.

PISCANO: I'm sorry . . .

PISCANO: behind my head. They trust that scumbag, I don't. Right now, the way I feel, I'll hit the two of them [Nance, and Green, another mobster] in the head with a fuckin' shovel.

PISCANO'S MOTHER: All right, take it easy now, take it easy.

PISCANO: Mom, I'm sorry, they're beatin' me left and right. *(knocking down some bottles of olive oil)* Ma, I'm sorry. I'm all upset.

PISCANO'S MOTHER: *(tapping the counter)* I know, but that's enough.

PISCANO: You know—You know—You know what they're doin' to me?

PISCANO'S MOTHER: I know it, I know it.

PISCANO: I can't take this no more. Back and forth, back and forth.

PISCANO'S MOTHER: Take it easy, though.

PISCANO: All right, all right. But I—I—

PISCANO'S MOTHER: You'll get a heart attack like that.

PISCANO: You know, I—I'm too upset right now. And—An end has to be put to this.

Interior. Post office, small room. Kansas City. Behind a window overlooking the grocery store are two FBI agents listening to Piscano's conversation.

PISCANO: *(over transmitter)* . . . did years ago, start kickin' ass, I—I'll do it, and I'll use the goddamn shovel! I mean, I . . .

Catherine Scorsese, Vinny Vella, and Martin Scorsese on the set of *Casino*, 1995.

(We see an agent looking out of the window with a pair of binoculars.)

PISCANO'S MOTHER: *(over transmitter)* You are right.

(The other agent, with headphones, is seated at a desk by a tape recorder, writing.)

PISCANO: *(over transmitter)* . . . everything's comin' out of my pocket. I gotta pay for all these trips back and forth, back and forth.

PISCANO'S MOTHER: *(over transmitter)* You are right. What can I . . .

Interior. Washington FBI office.

PISCANO'S MOTHER: *(on tape recorder)* . . . tell you.

(The camera tilts down an American flag to reveal the tape now being transcribed by an FBI stenographer.)

ACE: *(voice-over)* Would you believe that such a thing could happen?

PISCANO: *(on tape recorder)* I'm in this to make money, not to lose money. And I—I—

ACE: *(voice-over)* Every FBI man across the country had their ears open now.

PISCANO'S MOTHER: *(on tape recorder)* Then do it the way you want. What can I tell you?

ACE: *(voice-over)* I mean . . . Piscano, this guy basically . . . sunk the whole world.

PISCANO'S MOTHER: *(on tape recorder)* That's the way people are. There are some that are good and some that are bad.

(Martin Scorsese and Nicholas Pileggi: Casino)

MOVIE ROLES

Catherine Scorsese

It's Not Just You, Murray!, 1964: Mother

Who's That Knocking at My Door?, 1969: J.R.'s mother

Mean Streets, 1973: Woman in apartment hallway

Italianamerican, 1974: Main subject of documentary

New York, New York, 1977: Bystander

The King of Comedy, 1982: Rupert's mother

Easy Money, 1983 (James Signorelli, director): Joe Pesci's mother

Wiseguys, 1983 (Brian De Palma, director)

Prizzi's Honor, 1985 (John Huston, director): Wedding guest

The Color of Money, 1986: Bystander

GoodFellas, 1990: Tommy's mother

Cape Fear, 1991: Fruit stand customer

Godfather III, 1993 (Francis Ford Coppola, director): Neighborhood woman

The Age of Innocence, 1993: Arriving immigrant

Men Lie, 1994 (John Gallagher, director). Unreleased

Casino, 1995: Piscano's mother

DROPPED SCENES

Taxi Driver, 1975

Jungle Fever, 1991 (Spike Lee, director)

Charles Scorsese

It's Not Just You, Murray!, 1964

Italianamerican, 1974: Main subject of documentary

New York, New York, 1977: Bystander

Raging Bull, 1980: Charlie

Little Miss Marker, 1980 (Walter Benjamin, director):
     Presser in dry-cleaning store

Desperately Seeking Susan, 1985 (Susan Seidelman, director):
     Bystander

Prizzi's Honor, 1985 (John Huston, director): Wedding guest

The Color of Money, 1986: Bystander

Moonstruck, 1987 (Norman Jewison, director): Customer in
     Italian grocery store

GoodFellas, 1990: Vinnie

Cape Fear, 1991: Fruit stand customer

Godfather III, 1993 (Francis Ford Coppola, director):
     Neighborhood man

The Age of Innocence, 1993: Arriving immigrant

DROPPED SCENES

The King of Comedy, 1982

Jungle Fever, 1991 (Spike Lee, director)

All movies are directed by Martin Scorsese unless otherwise indicated.

ACKNOWLEDGMENTS

Special thanks to my co-writer Georgia Downard, my sister-in-law Fanny di Giovanni, and my friend Susan Bruno, without whom this book would not have been possible.

For all their help, I'd like to thank Thelma Schoonmaker, Raffaele Donato, Margaret Bodde, Kim Sockwell, and particularly Deanna Avery at Cappa Productions; my lawyer Allan Arrow; Helen Morris, Wynn Dan, Sean Abbott, Eva Burt, Benjamin Dreyer, Susan M. S. Brown, and Pamela Cannon at Random House.

Most of all, thank you to my sons Frank and Martin for their love and encouragement.

CATHERINE SCORSESE

Thank you to Fanny di Giovanni for her enormous help in collecting, annotating, and finally helping me to test the recipes for this book. Her unfailing generosity and sense of humor made our task easier and so much more enjoyable. Thank you also to Susan Bruno, whose wonderful organization and infinite sense of calm kept all of us focused and on course. Her assistance was invaluable.

Thank you to Martin Scorsese for his guidance and insight. And finally, many thanks to Catherine Scorsese for lovingly accepting me into her family and allowing me to peek into her life. I came away richer for the experience and will be forever grateful.

GEORGIA DOWNARD

ILLUSTRATIONS

INDEX

CHICKEN AND MEAT

FISH AND SHELLFISH

VEGETABLES AND EGGS

ABOUT THE AUTHORS

CATHERINE SCORSESE, the daughter of Sicilian immigrants, was born on Elizabeth Street in New York's Little Italy. It was there that she met her husband, Charles. Catherine worked in the garment business while raising her two sons, Frank and Martin; later she enjoyed success playing small parts in Martin's movies, including *Mean Streets, GoodFellas,* and *Casino,* and cooking for the cast and crew on the sets. She has also appeared in Francis Ford Coppola's *Godfather III* and Susan Seidelman's *Desperately Seeking Susan.*

GEORGIA DOWNARD is the culinary director for the Food Channel Network. She has worked on all the *Gourmet* cookbooks, and she is the author of *The Big Carrot Book* and *The Big Broccoli Book.* She lives in New York City with her two children.

ABOUT THE TYPE

This book was set in Baskerville, a typeface which was designed by John Baskerville, an amateur printer and typefounder, and cut for him by John Handy in 1750. The type became popular again when The Lanston Monotype Corporation of London revived the classic Roman face in 1923. The Mergenthaler Linotype Company in England and the United States cut a version of Baskerville in 1931, making it one of the most widely used typefaces today.